THE MOON'S CYCLICAL PHASES:

UNDERSTANDING THE RELATIONSHIP BETWEEN THE EARTH, SUN AND MOON

Astronomy Beginners' Guide Grade 4 |
Children's Astronomy & Space Books

BABY PROFESSOR
EDUCATION KIDS

First Edition, 2020

Published in the United States by Speedy Publishing LLC, 40 E Main Street, Newark, Delaware 19711 USA.

© 2020 Baby Professor Books, an imprint of Speedy Publishing LLC

Baby Professor Books are available at special discounts when purchased in bulk for industrial and sales-promotional use. For details contact our Special Sales Team at Speedy Publishing LLC, 40 E Main Street, Newark, Delaware 19711 USA. Telephone (888) 248-4521 Fax: (210) 519-4043.

10 9 8 7 6 * 5 4 3 2 1

Print Edition: 9781541978126
Digital Edition: 9781541978256

See the world in pictures. Build your knowledge in style.
www.speedypublishing.com

TABLE OF CONTENTS

Have you ever wondered what it would be like to visit the Moon? A few people do! The first person to walk on the Moon was Neil Armstrong in 1969. Six lunar landings would follow, with the last one taking place in 1972.

The first person to walk on the Moon was Neil Armstrong in 1969.

Of all the natural objects in our solar system, the Moon is the closest one to the Earth. It orbits the Earth and has different effects on our planet. This book will discuss the unique and fascinating information about the Moon, including its phases, its size, its location, and its relationship with the Earth and Sun.

Of all the natural objects in our solar system, the Moon is the closest one to the Earth.

THE EARTH'S
NATURAL SATELLITE

A satellite is something that orbits, or goes around, another object. It is also used to describe objects that have been constructed by people on Earth and sent into space to orbit. Satellites are held into place by gravity. Since the Moon was not made by humans, it is a natural satellite. While the Earth has only one Moon, some planets have many Moons. Others have none.

A satellite is something that orbits, or goes around, another object.

The Moon is approximately 239,000 miles or 384,000 Kilometers away from the Earth. Since it does not orbit the Earth in a perfect circle, at its closest point, it is about 221,500 miles away, and at its furthest, it is 252,700 miles away. The point where it is closest is called the lunar perigee. The furthest point of the Moon from the Earth is called its apogee.

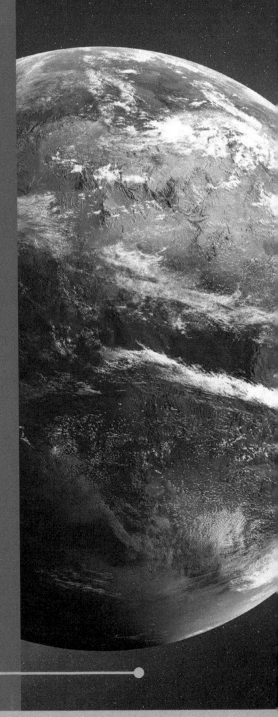

The Moon is approximately 239,000 miles or 384,000 Kilometers away from the Earth.

INTERESTING MOON FACTS:

The amount of gravity that an object creates is affected by how much mass it has. Since the Earth is made up of more material than the Moon, it has the stronger gravity. The Moon is only about a quarter the size of the Earth.

The Moon is only about a quarter the size of the Earth.

Thus, the gravitational pull of the Moon is too weak to affect the entire Earth. However, it can cause water to move. It is the gravity of the Moon pulling on the Earth which causes tides on the Earth to rise and fall.

The gravity of the Moon causes tides on the Earth to rise and fall.

The Earth pulls everything toward it that is within its gravitational field. This is why we do not float off into outer space. However, the Moon does not fall to the Earth. The reason is that the Moon is always moving. The movement that the Moon makes around and around the Earth keeps it from falling into our planet.

The reason why we do not float off into outer space is because of the Earth's gravity.

Galileo Galilei, a famous Italian astronomer born in 1564 and who is commonly known as Galileo, used to study the Moon. He discovered large areas which looked shadowed. He guessed that these areas were seas of water. He was wrong. These areas are dark because of hardened rock from volcanic eruptions. However, when naming features of the Moon we still call such an area a sea, or the Latin term for it, mare.

Ancient statue of Galileo Galilei in Florence, Italy

THE NEAR SIDE OF THE MOON:

The Moon orbits the Earth, but it also revolves around its own axis. Since the Moon orbits the Earth and revolves around its axis in about the same amount of time, we can only see one side of the Moon from the Earth. We call the side of the Moon that we can see, the side that is always facing the Earth, the near side of the Moon.

The side of the Moon that is always facing the Earth is called the near side of the Moon.

We can see the near side of the Moon because the Moon reflects light from the Sun. The Moon does not produce light itself. Without a reflection of the Sun, we would not be able to see the Moon like we do!

Without the Sun, we would not be able to see the Moon.

THE FAR SIDE OF THE MOON:

For many millennia, no one knew what the far side or the side of the Moon that is away from the Earth, looked like. It was assumed that it looked much the same as the near side. This assumption was proven to be wrong in 1969.

The far side of the Moon is the hemisphere of the Moon that always faces away from Earth.

In 1969, the Luna 3 was launched by the Soviets to travel to the far side of the Moon. It took some remarkably interesting photos which showed that the far side of the Moon is considerably different than the side which is visible from Earth!

Luna 3 was a Soviet spacecraft launched in 1959 as part of the Luna programme.

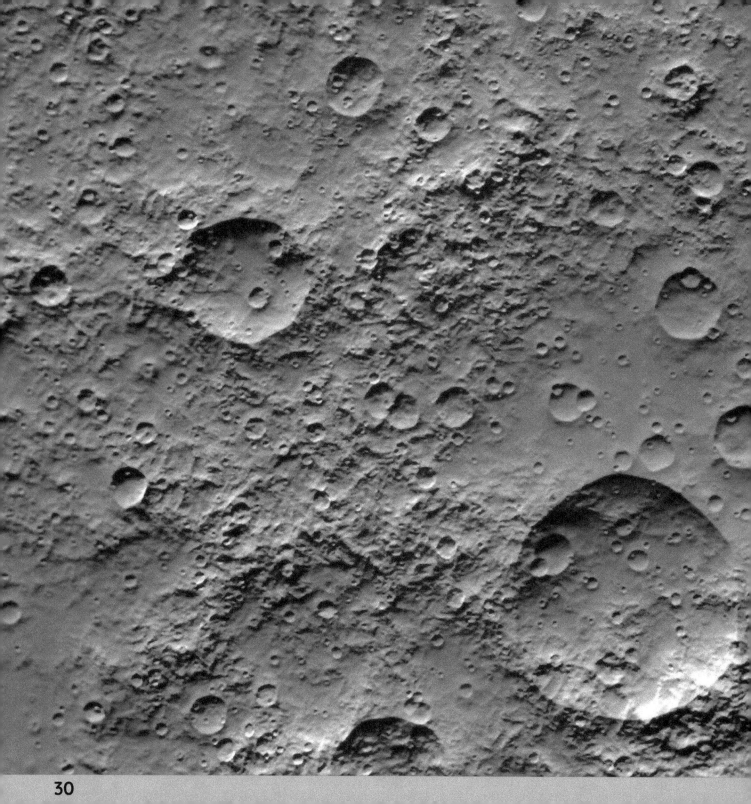

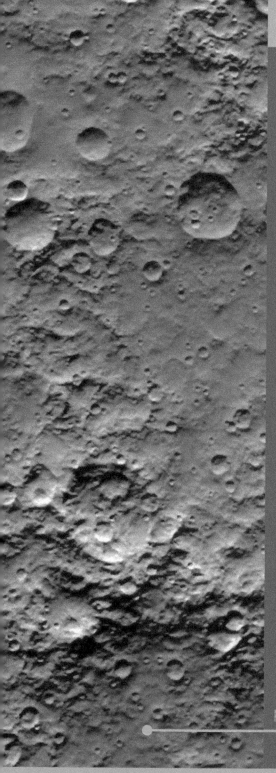

While the near side has many plains, the far side of the Moon does not. Instead, the far side is covered with numerous craters. Scientists now think that these craters were caused by objects like asteroids or comets forcefully going into the Moon. They went there rather than into the surface of the Earth.

The far side of the moon is covered with numerous craters possibly from asteroids or comets.

THE PHASES OF
THE MOON

We know the true source of the Moon being able to shine – a reflection of the Sun, but why does it have phases? How come we sometimes see a half-moon, a crescent moon, or a full moon? The reason for this phenomenon relates to the rotations of the Moon, the Earth, and the Sun. The positions of the different objects to each other affects how much we can see.

The reason why the Moon has phases relates to the rotations of the Moon, the Earth, and the Sun.

CAUSES OF THE PHASES OF THE MOON:

The phases of the Moon make a complete cycle in almost a month. The full moon can be seen once in a twenty-nine and a half-day period. When there is a full moon, it means that the Earth is centered between the Moon and the Sun. As a result, the Sun hits the near side of the Moon which we, from Earth, can see entirely lit up.

When there is a full moon, it means that the Earth is centered between the Moon and the Sun.

As the Moon revolves around the Earth, it can become harder to see the half of the Moon that is lit up due to the rays of the Sun. When we only see a sliver of the Moon that is lit up, we call it the crescent moon. When the side of the Moon that is reflecting the Sun is not towards the Earth, we see no moon at all. We call this the new moon. It is important to remember that half of the Moon is always bright from the sunlight; we simply cannot always see it from our position on Earth.

When we only see a sliver of the Moon that is lit up, we call it the crescent moon.

THE FIRST PART OF THE LUNAR CYCLE:

The lunar cycle describes the phases that the Moon goes through as we see it from Earth. If we begin with the new moon, the Moon is between the Earth and the Sun. As a result, we cannot see the light that shines on the Moon since it is blocked from us. It seems as if there is no Moon in the sky at all.

A new moon happens when the Moon is between the Earth and the Sun.

First
quarter

Next comes the crescent moon which occurs when the Moon has moved so that it is not directly between the Sun and the Earth. We can see just a sliver of its sunlit half. As days pass, the Moon will continue to move, and we will see the first quarter-moon. The quarter-moon shows us half of the lit side of the Moon.

The quarter-moon shows us half of the lit side of the Moon.

The phases of the Moon between the crescent and the first quarter-moon are called the waxing crescent. If the Moon is waxing, we can see more of it. When about three-quarters of the Moon is visible, it is called the waxing gibbous. Eventually, the Moon will be visible as a full moon.

If the Moon is waxing, we can see more of it.

Waxing
crescent

Waxing
gibbous

Waning
gibbous

Waning
crescent

THE SECOND PART OF THE LUNAR CYCLE:

The second part of the lunar cycle follows the Sun as it wanes. If the Moon is waning, it means that we are seeing less and less of it as we head towards a new moon. It is like the first lunar phases, except that it happens backwards.

If the Moon is waning, it means that we are seeing less and less of it as we head towards a new moon.

First, we will have the full moon; then we will have the waning gibbous moon. The last quarter-moon comes next where, once again, we only see half of the sunlit portion of the Moon. The Moon will continue to wane until we have another crescent moon. Finally, the Moon will be back where it started, and we will have a new moon.

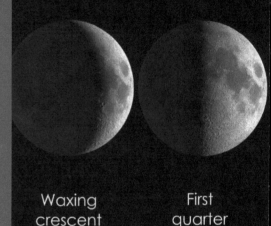

Waxing crescent

First quarter

The phases of the Moon.

Waxing gibbous   Full moon   Waning gibbous   Third quarter   Waning crescent

MOON PHASES

ECLIPSES

An eclipse is what happens when we cannot see something because it is blocked by another object. An eclipse can happen when the Moon, the Earth, and the Sun line up in just the right way that, from Earth, we cannot see either the Moon or the Sun properly.

An eclipse is what happens when we cannot see something because it is blocked by another object.

Historically, an eclipse could cause a great deal of awe and fear. People did not understand what could cause the Sun to darken or the Moon to change color. Now scientists know that this is caused by the orbit of the Moon around the Earth and the Earth around the Sun. Scientists can even predict when it will happen.

Scientists can even predict when an eclipse will happen.

56

A SOLAR ECLIPSE:

When the Earth and the Sun are on either side of the Moon, so that the Moon is in the center of the two, the result is a Solar eclipse. A solar eclipse occurs because the Moon blocks sunlight from reaching the Earth. The Moon's shadow will also make the sky seem darker.

A solar eclipse occurs because the Moon blocks sunlight from reaching the Earth.

If the light from the Sun is completely blocked, we will be able to see the Moon with a ring of fire around it. The ring of fire is the gases from the Sun that the Moon cannot block out. Since the Earth and the Moon are both still moving, the phenomenon ends in a few minutes. If the Sun is entirely blocked, it is called a total eclipse. If the Sun is not entirely blocked, it is called a partial eclipse.

The ring of fire is the gases from the Sun that the Moon cannot block out.

Whether or not you will see an eclipse can also depend upon where you are on the Earth. Some people may only see a partial eclipse, while others will see a total eclipse. Some may see nothing at all. Only those who live in an area where the Moon's shadow will be, will be able to see the total eclipse. People just outside that will see a partial one. Since looking at a solar eclipse can damage your eyes, it is not a good idea to look directly at one unless you have the proper eye protection.

A kid wearing eye protection glasses before looking at a solar eclipse.

A LUNAR ECLIPSE:

A lunar eclipse is what happens when the Earth blocks sunlight from reaching the Moon. This means that the shadow of the Earth is on the Moon. The Moon will not, however, look entirely darkened. Rather, it will glow with a burnt orange color. This color occurs because some light does reach the Moon as it reflects off the gases that surround the Earth. Like solar eclipses, a lunar eclipse can be total or partial. However, unlike solar eclipses, it is safe to watch a lunar eclipse directly.

During a lunar eclipse, the Moon will glow with a burnt orange color.

The Moon is Earth's only natural satellite. It affects our tides and helps protect us from objects in outer space. Many interesting phenomena in our world exist because of the way the Moon and the Earth rotate around the Sun. The phases of the Moon are determined by how much of the sunlit Moon we can see as it orbits around the Earth.

The Moon is Earth's only natural satellite.

Eclipses also happen when the Earth, the Moon, and the Sun line up in just the right place that either the Earth or the Moon blocks out light. Eclipses can be lunar or solar, partial, or total.

Solar and Lunar eclipses.

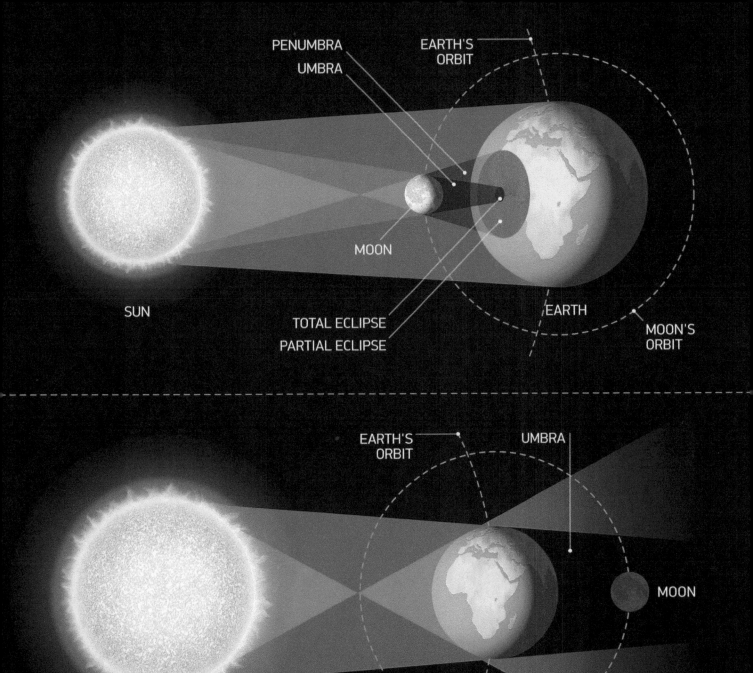

PENUMBRA

UMBRA

EARTH'S ORBIT

MOON

SUN

TOTAL ECLIPSE

PARTIAL ECLIPSE

EARTH

MOON'S ORBIT

EARTH'S ORBIT

UMBRA

MOON

SUN

MOON'S ORBIT

EARTH

PENUMBRA

67

Whether or not we can see them, also depends on where we are on the Earth. To learn more about space, the Moon, and our solar system, look for more Baby Professor books!

A camera view of an ongoing eclipse.

Visit

www.speedypublishing.com

To view and download free content on your
favorite subject and browse our catalog of new
and exciting books for readers of all ages.

Printed in the USA
CPSIA information can be obtained
at www.ICGtesting.com
LVHW050440270923
758034LV00004B/68